Written by Pamela Hickman • Illustrated by Heather Collins

THE KIDS CANADIAN

Bird

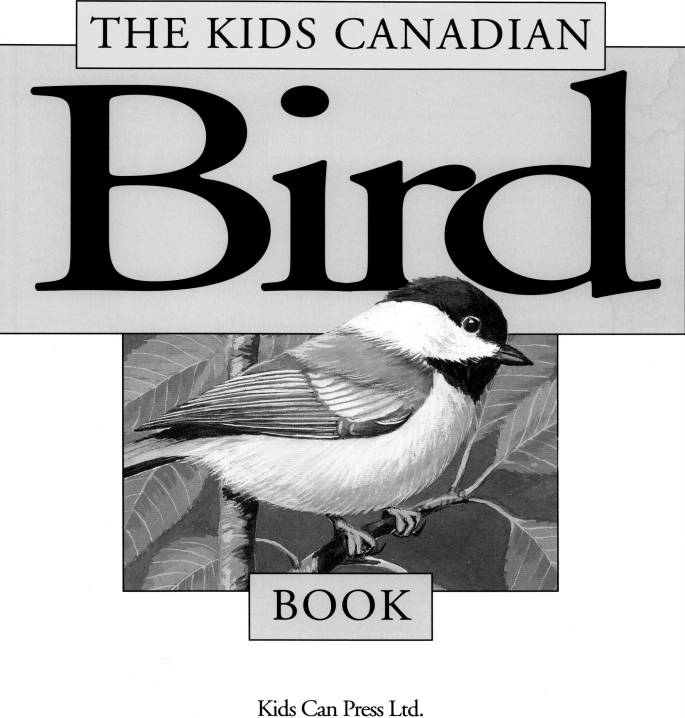

BOOK

Kids Can Press Ltd.

Toronto

Kids Can Press Ltd. acknowledges with appreciation the assistance of the Canada Council and the Ontario Arts Council in the production of this book.

Canadian Cataloguing in Publication Data

Hickman, Pamela
　　The kids Canadian bird book

(Kids Canadian nature series)
Includes index.
ISBN 1-55074-196-9 (bound) ISBN 1-55074-334-1 (pbk.)

1. Birds — Canada — Juvenile literature.
I. Collins, Heather. II. Title.
III. Series: Hickman, Pamela. Kids Canadian nature series.

QL685.H53　　1995　　j598'.2971　　C95-930639-0

Kids Can Press Ltd.
29 Birch Avenue
Toronto, Ontario, Canada
M4V 1E2

Edited by Trudee Romanek
Series editor: Laurie Wark
Designed by Blair Kerrigan/Glyphics

Printed in Hong Kong
by Wing King Tong Company Limited

PA 96 0 9 8 7 6 5 4 3 2 1

Acknowledgements

Thanks to Valerie Hussey at Kids Can Press who suggested the Kids Canadian Nature Series and, even better, asked me to write it. I'd like to thank my editor, Trudee Romanek, for her patience and amazing "text shrinking" abilities throughout the series. Thanks also to Blair Kerrigan for his great series design and to Heather Collins for bringing the books to life. I'm also grateful to my in-laws, Jack and Juliet Hickman, for taking care of my three children while my husband and I ventured to the Gaspé to view the gannet colony and other sea birds, firsthand.

For James, Catherine and Rebecca Hunter
PH

CONTENTS

Meet a bird

What is your favourite bird? Maybe it is a loon, a chickadee or a woodpecker. Canada is home to all these birds and more. Whether you live in the city or the country, you will find plenty of birds to watch and listen to. In this book you will find out about birds from coast to coast and discover how you can become a bird watcher and attract birds to your backyard, balcony or cottage. Start your bird watching adventure by meeting the birds on these pages. These birds look very different from each other, but they have a lot in common.

Many birds migrate, or travel, long distances in search of food.

All birds have a beak, two wings, two legs and a tail.

All birds have feathers, and they are the only animals that have them.

AMAZING BIRDS

Canada's smallest bird is the Calliope Hummingbird, which is found in the mountains of British Columbia and southwestern Alberta. Its body is about as long as a stick of gum and it weighs less than some insects.

All birds lay eggs, and most birds build nests and take special care of their young.

Beaks, feet and feathers

All birds have a beak, two feet and feathers, but why do they all look so different? Bird bodies are adapted to the different habitats they live in. Water birds may eat fish, while woodland birds eat seeds or insects. These birds have specially shaped beaks to help them eat their preferred foods. A bird's feet may be used for catching food or for getting around in its habitat. Feathers are important, too — they keep the bird warm and dry, they help it fly and they are specially coloured to attract a mate or to hide the bird from predators or prey.

Great Blue Heron
Its large beak is perfect for spearing fish and frogs. The long, widely spread toes are designed for balance and for walking through shallow water.

Red-breasted Merganser
The sawtoothed edge on its beak holds on to fish. Its feathers are waterproofed with natural oils. The webbed feet help it swim and dive.

Ruby-throated Hummingbird

The straw-shaped beak fits easily into bell-shaped flowers and its long tongue laps up the sweet nectar.

Bay-breasted Warbler

A pointed, tweezerlike beak is great for picking up insects.

AMAZING BIRDS

The Northern Shrike is a robin-sized songbird that feeds on small mammals and birds. Its beak is perfect for catching its prey, but the shrike's small feet are too weak to hold it. Instead, the shrike sticks its prey on large thorns in trees or shrubs, or on barbed wire, to hold the food while it is eating.

Snowy Owl

A strong, hooked beak is useful for carrying food and tearing it into pieces. The sharp claws, called talons, are designed to catch and kill small animals like lemmings and mice. In the Arctic ice and snow, white feathers make it easier to sneak up on prey.

Pine Grosbeak (male)

The thick, strong beak is perfect for crunching and cracking seeds. Small feet are good for perching. Dull-coloured feathers help the female hide while she sits on her nest. The male's red colour helps it attract a mate.

Bird families

A puffin lays only one egg each year, but a Ruffed Grouse may lay twelve eggs. All birds lay eggs, but they don't all lay the same number. Once the eggs are laid they must be kept warm, or incubated, until they hatch. Usually the female bird sits on the nest while the male hunts for food and feeds her. The female has an area of bare skin called a brood patch on her stomach. This bare patch lets the adult's warm body lay directly on the eggs to keep them warm. Incubation can take from 11 to 80 days, depending on the kind of bird.

Songbirds like Blue Jays are naked and helpless when they hatch. They have to be kept warm by the mother bird until their first, fluffy down feathers grow. The babies of ducks, geese and grouse, however, are born with feathers, and they can walk and feed themselves soon after they hatch.

tanager

Each baby bird has a sharp knob on its beak called an egg tooth. When hatching day arrives, this is used to break the shell open from the inside.

mallard

Baby birds are always hungry, and both parents work hard to find food for their young. Most land birds feed their young insects, but baby sea birds eat mashed up fish.

As the young birds grow, they soon become too big for the nest. Now it's time to leave home, or fledge. Even after a bird leaves the nest, its parents still feed it on the ground for a week or two while the fledgling learns to fly and look after itself.

herons

Do you have a bird in your pocket? Four different birds appear on Canadian money. Try to find out what they are.

Northern Gannet

Barn Swallow

Great Crested Flycatcher

Red-eyed Vireo

Bird homes

If you were a mother bird, you would raise your family where the eggs and babies would be safe from danger. Some birds build nests in trees or shrubs, on the sides of buildings or cliffs, on the ground or even underground. Not all birds build nests, though. Razorbills lay their eggs on bare rock, while the Eastern Screech-owl uses an old woodpecker hole for its eggs. Here are some more amazing bird homes.

Common Murres breed in huge groups, or colonies, on cliffs along Canada's Atlantic and Pacific coasts. Each female lays only one egg on the bare rock of a cliff ledge. The egg is pear-shaped so that if it rolls, it will move in a circle and won't fall off the ledge.

Eared Grebes build their nests on
floating marsh plants in the shallow
waters of prairie lakes and ponds.
The nest is safe from land enemies
like skunks, and the babies can easily
step out of the nest for a swim.

Can you guess where
Chimney Swifts nest? In
chimneys, of course. These
birds rest and nest on the
walls inside chimneys.
Swifts use their saliva to
hold their shelflike nest of
twigs together and to stick
it onto the chimney wall.

The Northern
Oriole weaves
plant fibres, hair
and twine into a
deep, baglike nest.
The nest hangs
down from a high
branch in a tree
and even sways on
windy days, like a
cradle for baby birds.

AMAZING BIRDS

Cowbirds don't build nests
or look after their young.
They lay their eggs in the
nests of other birds and fly
off, leaving a stranger to
raise the baby cowbirds.

Make a bird house

Make a bird feel at home by building this simple bird house. You may get a family of sparrows, Tree Swallows, wrens or chickadees for neighbours.

You'll need:

a 2-L milk carton, rinsed out

scissors

2 nails

50 cm of thin wire

dry leaves or grasses

waterproof tape, such as packing or electrical tape

a hammer

1. Ask an adult to help you cut out a circle 4 cm wide, about 5 cm below the bend in the carton.

2. On the opposite side of the carton, use a nail to poke two holes. Place the top hole about one-third of the way down from the bend and the second hole about two-thirds of the way down.

3. Thread the wire through the top hole, down the carton on the inside and out of the bottom hole.

4. Put some dry leaves or grasses in the bottom of the carton to help attract birds.

5. Use waterproof tape to close the top of the milk carton tightly.

6. In the early spring, find a pole or tree in an open area. Hammer in your nails about 30 cm apart, one above the other. Wrap one end of the wire around each nail to hold the bird house firmly to the tree or pole.

7. Watch the birds nesting but remember not to get too close to the nest or to disturb the birds. If the birds don't use your house the first year, leave it up and try again next year.

A helping hand

In early spring you can offer birds a helping hand by hanging nesting materials in the open on a tree or shrub. Try bits of string and yarn, hair from your hairbrush, small scraps of cloth or lint from the clean-out tray in the clothes dryer. Watch as the birds gather the supplies and fly off to weave their nests.

Birds in winter

How do you stay warm during cold and snowy winters? You probably spend more time indoors and dress in extra layers of warm clothes when you go outside. Have you ever wondered how winter birds keep warm? Birds are experts at winter survival and they have taught us a lot about staying warm in winter.

Take a good look at birds in winter — do they sometimes look fatter than usual? On cold days, birds fluff up to trap air in their feathers. The air acts as insulation to keep the birds warm. The Gray, or Canada, Jay can puff up to almost three times its normal size in winter. When you wear a fluffy, down-filled jacket, you are wearing feathers, too — down is really tiny bird feathers. Some birds grow up to 1000 extra feathers in winter to stay warm — like putting on a winter coat. The ptarmigan even grows extra feathers on its toes! These feathers act like snowshoes, helping the bird to walk over the snow without sinking into it.

Huddling together in a group is a good way to stay warm. Chickadees gather in tree holes and starlings roost together in sheltered areas to share body heat.

Ptarmigan are the only birds in Canada that turn white in the winter to match the snow. This is called camouflage, and it helps the birds hide from their enemies. To keep from starving, ptarmigan change their diet in winter and eat buds and twigs instead of insects.

Ruffed Grouse survive cold winter nights by diving into snow banks to keep warm. The air trapped in the snow acts like insulation to keep the birds warm. Snow Buntings, Common Redpolls and other small birds also shelter under the snow where they are warm and hidden from enemies.

Feed the birds

Finding food in winter is just as important for birds as staying warm. In fact, the more birds eat, the easier it is for them to stay warm. That's because food gives birds the energy they need to heat their bodies. You can help your local birds by making a bird feeder and keeping it full of food all winter long.

You'll need:

a plastic 4-L pop bottle, with lid

scissors

a stick (about 25 cm long and as thick as a pencil)

thin wire

bird seed

1. Rinse out the pop bottle. Ask an adult to cut an opening on one side of the bottle, about 7 cm wide and 10 cm long. Make the opening towards the top half of the bottle.

2. With the sharp point of the scissors, carefully poke a hole into the bottle about 2 cm below the bottom of the opening. Poke another hole directly across from this one on the other side of the bottle.

3. Slide your stick into the two holes so that it is balanced in your feeder. Birds will use the stick as a perch.

4. Wrap one end of a piece of wire tightly around the neck of the bottle and tie the other end to the branch of a tree so your feeder hangs freely. Hang your feeder where you can watch it from a window and where you can easily reach it for refilling.

5. Fill the feeder up to the opening with bird seed. A mixture of corn, sunflower seeds, unsalted peanuts and millet will keep every bird happy.

A summer bird feeder

Fruit-eating birds such as robins, waxwings and orioles will love this juicy, summertime feeder. Thread a wooden shish-kebab stick (available at grocery and kitchenware stores) with raisins, grapes, cherries, a partly-peeled orange with both ends cut off, and any other fruits you have around. Tie a long piece of string or thin wire to each end of the stick and hang it from a tree branch or clothesline.

Bird migration

As the days get colder, many Canadian birds head south to find food. Insect and nectar-feeding birds like warblers and hummingbirds have nothing to eat in the winter, since the insects are either dead or hibernating, and flowers are gone, too. Water birds also migrate because their food and homes become covered with ice and snow.

Birds usually leave about the same time each year, in late summer or fall, and return each spring. Why do they come back? Birds return to Canada because there is more food and space for nesting and less competition from other birds. Smaller birds, like warblers, usually migrate at night when they are safe from predators. Large birds, such as geese, travel during the day.

Not all migrating birds leave the country. Arctic nesters such as Snow Buntings, redpolls and tree sparrows find food and shelter in southern Canada. The Clark's Nutcracker simply leaves its Rocky Mountain home in the fall and heads down to the warmer valley for winter.

Bird banding

How do scientists find out about where birds migrate and what they do? Bird banders catch birds and attach a numbered band on a leg of each bird before letting it go. If the bird is caught again somewhere else, the number on the band will tell banders where and when it was banded. This information helps researchers learn many things about birds, including their migration patterns and how long they live.

If you see a wild bird with a band on its leg, try to read the band number with your binoculars. If you find a dead banded bird, ask an adult to help you remove the band. Write down the band number, what kind of bird it is (if you know), the date when you saw it (or found it) and where, and your name and address. Send the band and the information to: Bird-banding Office, Canadian Wildlife Service, Ottawa, Ontario K1A 0H3. They will send you information on where and when the bird was banded, and who banded it.

AMAZING BIRDS

The Arctic Tern is the world's champion long-distance migrant. At the end of summer it leaves its Arctic nesting grounds and heads southward to the Antarctic Circle. Arctic Terns nesting in the eastern Canadian Arctic fly across the Atlantic Ocean before heading south along the coasts of Europe and Africa.

Bird songs

You may have heard a rooster crow at dawn, but have you listened to the choir of birds that sing as the sun is rising? Many birds start the morning with a song and continue singing off and on all day. They use songs to defend a breeding territory and to attract a mate. Birds also sing when they are angry, frightened or hungry.

In early spring, a male bird claims an area as his breeding territory where he and his mate will nest and raise their young. To keep other male birds away, he perches in high places such as treetops or rooftops, and sings loudly. The song means "no trespassing." When a female is nearby, the male changes his tune to attract a mate.

When you walk through the woods it's often hard to see the birds hidden among the leaves. You can hear their different songs, though, and with some practice, you'll begin to recognize a few birds by their voices. An easy way of remembering bird songs is by thinking up words that fit the song's pattern. The clear whistle of the White-throated Sparrow sounds like the bird is saying "I love Canada, Canada, Canada." Other birds, such as the Killdeer, Eastern Phoebe, Black-capped Chickadee and Whip-poor-will sound as if they are singing their own names. Blue Jays, cowbirds and grackles sometimes sound like squeaky clotheslines, and the Gray Catbird actually sounds like a meowing cat.

"I love Canada, Canada, Canada."

"chickadee-dee"

"meow"

Loon-y tunes

Try bird watching with a tape recorder as well as binoculars. If you play a recording of a specific bird song, such as a loon, outdoors, you may get a loon to call back or to fly into view. With some practice, you can start imitating bird songs yourself. Repeat the songs you hear outdoors until they sound right and the birds start calling back.

Beginner bird watching

Wherever you are in Canada, you will find birds to watch. You will see them resting on telephone wires and trees, soaring overhead, swimming or wading in the water. With over 500 different kinds of birds in Canada, you may wonder how to tell them apart. You can recognize birds by their shape, colour, size, special body parts, markings and songs. If you see a bird with very long legs, you know that it is probably a wader or shorebird that feeds along the edge of the water.

This basic checklist will help you decide what general type of bird you are looking at. Then you can use a field guide to identify it.

size

shape

beaks

tails

colour and markings

Size

Is the bird small like a chickadee, medium-sized like a robin or as large as a pigeon?

Shape

Does the bird have a plump body like a robin or is it slender like a swallow?

Special Body Parts

What shape is the bird's beak?

Does the bird have long or short legs?

Is its tail long or short? What shape is it?

Are the bird's feet webbed, strongly hooked or small and weak?

Is there a crest on its head?

What shape are its wings?

Colour and Markings

What colour is the bird?

Can you see spots or stripes on the bird's breast?

Is there an eye stripe, wing bars, tail stripe or other patch of colour?

Movement

What is the bird doing when you see it?

Is it swimming, diving or wading in water?

Is it hopping up a tree or climbing down head first?

Does it glide through the air, hover in one spot or fly up and down like a roller coaster?

Location

What habitat, such as a forest, lake or meadow, is the bird in when you see it?

What part of the country is it in? Check the range maps in a field guide to find out what birds you can expect near you.

Bird watching tips

- Always have binoculars and a field guide handy.

- Take some bird seed in your pocket. Chickadees will often feed from your hand if you stand very still.

- Be as quiet as possible.

- Make a bird bath and bird feeder to attract birds to your yard.

- Keep a record of the birds that visit your feeder and bird bath and compare your lists each year.

Sea birds

Some birds spend their lives out on the ocean and return to land to nest. Canada has the longest coastline of any country in the world and our three oceans — the Pacific, Atlantic and Arctic — provide homes for millions of sea birds.

Sea birds are well adapted to their special habitat. Their toes are webbed like flippers to help them swim. Puffins, murres and guillemots also use their short, narrow wings to swim underwater. To stay warm in the cold water, sea birds have a thick layer of short, fluffy down feathers next to their bodies. They also have a special oil gland at the base of their tails. The birds spread the oil on their feathers when they are preening to make them waterproof.

Most sea birds nest in huge groups called colonies. The birds crowd together in the best nesting areas near good food supplies, so more of them can survive. They are also safer nesting in colonies because there are many more eyes watching for enemies.

Murres are known as the penguins of the north. These black-and-white birds have short legs set far back on their bodies so they walk upright like penguins. Although both are expert swimmers, only murres can fly.

The Atlantic Puffin is sometimes called a sea parrot because of its large, colourful, striped beak. After breeding season is over, its beak gets smaller and duller.

Most birds incubate their eggs by sitting on them, but gannet parents take turns keeping their single egg warm with their feet. While one parent stays with the egg, the other goes hunting for fish and other sea animals. Nearly 50 000 of these birds live on Bonaventure Island in Quebec, North America's largest gannet colony.

Prairie birds

You may be used to seeing birds up in trees, but there are lots of birds in the open prairies, too. The grasslands and prairie sloughs (shallow, marshy ponds) are perfect habitats for many different birds. In fact, over half the ducks born in North America start their life in small prairie wetlands. Many of the birds in the prairie grasslands are sandy-coloured or brown, blending in well with the dry prairie. Even their eggs are light coloured with brown spots for camouflage.

Burrowing Owl
Small, long-legged Burrowing Owls live in the prairies. Their nests are built in underground burrows left by small prairie mammals. Unlike most other owls, Burrowing Owls are active during the day and night.

Sharp-tailed Grouse
Each spring, Sharp-tailed Grouse gather on their special prairie dancing grounds, where the males put on a great display of foot stomping and noise making to attract a mate. The males inflate their purple neck pouches like small balloons and make a low booming sound to attract females.

Swainson's Hawk

If you see a large, brown-and-white hawk perched on a roadside fence, it is probably a Swainson's Hawk — the most common hawk of the prairies. It feeds on the mice, gophers and large grasshoppers that live in the grasslands.

AMAZING BIRDS

The Prairie Warbler is not found in the prairies. It breeds in southern Ontario in dry, shrubby areas and sand-dune habitat.

Marbled Godwit

You can tell that the Marbled Godwit is a shorebird by its long legs and long, slender beak. This large bird comes to the prairies in summer to breed in the grasslands and feed at the edges of sloughs and lakes.

Ruddy Duck

This small diving duck breeds mainly in western Canada, especially in prairie lakes, ponds and sloughs. It weaves marsh plants into a nest hidden among the reeds and cattails.

Birds and you

Try to imagine a world without birds. You would miss their songs and pretty colours, but birds add much more to our world than that.

Birds are an important part of the wildlife food chain. Foxes, weasels, coyotes, mink, lynx, snakes and snapping turtles are some of the predators that feed on birds. Birds' eggs are also eaten by many animals such as raccoons and skunks. All these creatures, and many more, depend on birds for survival.

Plants depend on birds, too. Flowers make seeds, and then more flowers, when they are pollinated. Hummingbirds pollinate flowers when they visit them to feed on the nectar. Fruit-eating birds such as robins are great for spreading seeds around. Since these birds can't digest the seeds, they come out in the birds' droppings, often a long way from where the fruit was picked.

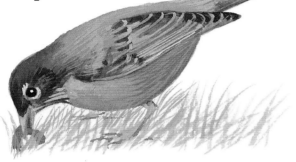

Birds are very important to farmers because they eat millions of insect pests and weed seeds that could damage crops. They also eat mosquitoes, blackflies and other nuisance insects.

Canada's provincial birds

Check the list below to find out what bird represents your province or territory.

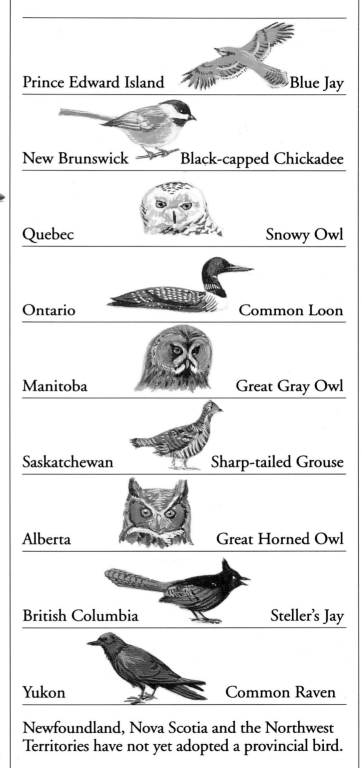

Prince Edward Island — Blue Jay

New Brunswick — Black-capped Chickadee

Quebec — Snowy Owl

Ontario — Common Loon

Manitoba — Great Gray Owl

Saskatchewan — Sharp-tailed Grouse

Alberta — Great Horned Owl

British Columbia — Steller's Jay

Yukon — Common Raven

Newfoundland, Nova Scotia and the Northwest Territories have not yet adopted a provincial bird.

Endangered birds

Imagine if a bulldozer knocked down your home. You'd have to find somewhere else to live. Many birds across the country have their homes destroyed each day as forests are cut down, wetlands are drained and grasslands are ploughed under for farms, roads and subdivisions. Oil spills and other pollution is another problem that threatens birds and their habitats. It's not always possible for birds to find new homes when theirs are destroyed. Loss of their habitat is endangering some birds.

When a species is endangered it means that something is killing it. If it isn't helped, all the birds of that species may die. When this happens, the species is extinct and is found nowhere in the world. The Labrador Duck, the Great Auk and the Passenger Pigeon are examples of extinct Canadian birds.

Labrador Duck

Endangered birds

These birds are listed as endangered in Canada.

	Bird	Location in Canada
1	Whooping Crane	NWT
2	Eskimo Curlew	NWT
3	Harlequin Duck (eastern population)	PQ, NF, NB, NS
4	Peregrine Falcon (*anatum*)	everywhere except PEI
5	Spotted Owl	BC
6	Mountain Plover	AB, SK
7	Piping Plover	everywhere except BC, NWT, YT
8	Loggerhead Shrike (eastern population)	MB, ON, PQ
9	Sage Thrasher	AB, BC, SK
10	Kirtland's Warbler	ON, PQ
11	Henslow's Sparrow	ON
12	Acadian Flycatcher	ON
13	King Rail	ON
14	Northern Bobwhite	ON

You can help

All across the country people are working together to save endangered birds. Peregrine Falcons are being reintroduced, Piping Plover nests are being guarded on New Brunswick beaches and the Grasslands National Park is protecting important bird habitats in Saskatchewan. You can be a friend to birds, too, and help make sure that no more species become endangered. Here's how.

- Make a bird feeder and remember to keep it full of food all winter long.

- Plant sunflowers, zinnias and other annual flowers in a garden or in pots. These plants produce lots of seeds and make great natural bird feeders in the winter.

- Build a bird house and put it up in early spring before the birds start nesting.

- Keep birds from crashing into a large window by making a black hawk silhouette from cardboard. Hang it outside the window.

- Make and sell bird houses and bird feeders to raise money for conservation groups that protect birds and their habitats. Advertise your campaign in a local newspaper.

Index

A
Arctic birds, 7, 18, 19
attracting a mate, 6, 7, 20, 26

B
baby birds, 8–9, 10–11
beaks, 6–7, 22, 25
bird banding, 19
bird bodies
  general features, 4, 6
  smallest, 5
  special features, 6–7, 22–23
  See also beaks, feathers, feet
bird families, 8–9
bird feeders, 16–17, 23, 31
bird homes, 10–11
bird house, 12–13, 31
bird songs, 20–21
birdwatching, 20–21, 22–23
breeding territory, 20
brood patch, 8

C
camouflage, 6, 7, 15, 26
colonies, 10, 24, 25

D
down feathers, 8, 14, 24

E
egg tooth, 8
eggs, 5, 8, 25, 28
  abandoned, 11, 26
  incubation, 8, 25
  special features, 10, 26
endangered species, 30–31
extinct species, 30

F
feathers, 4, 6–7, 8, 14, 24
feet, 6–7, 14, 25
fledglings, 9
flesh eaters, 6, 7, 9, 27
food, 6–7, 17, 18, 27, 29, 31
  for babies 9
  in winter, 15, 16–17, 18
food chains, 28, 29
fruit eaters, 17, 29

H
habitat, 6, 24–25, 26–27, 30, 31
hatching, 8
hummingbirds, 5, 7, 18, 29

I
incubation, 8, 25
insect eaters, 7, 9, 15, 18, 29

M
mate, attraction of, 6, 7, 20, 26
migration, 4, 18–19
  longest, 19

N
nectar eaters, 7, 18, 29
nests, 5, 10–11, 13, 26, 27

O
oil glands, 24
owls, 7, 10, 26

P
prairie birds, 26–27
predators of birds, 6, 11, 28
provincial birds, 29

S
sea birds, 9, 10, 24–25
seed eaters, 7, 29
shorebirds, 22, 27
smallest bird, 5

W
water birds, 6, 11, 18, 22, 26, 27
  See also sea birds
winter birds, 14–15, 18